Crashing Asphalt

Olivia Aguilar

BookLeaf Publishing

Presentation by *BookLeaf Publishing*

Web: www.bookleafpub.com

E-mail: info@bookleafpub.com

ISBN: 9789357441582

First edition 2023

DEDICATION

To the women who got me through this, thank you

Entwined Bodies

I know how it would've been
our love, our beings entwined
but it wasn't for this lifetime
so I hope that in my next body
your familiarity will awaken my soul sooner
telling me: it will be…

The Breath

Breathing says it all when words can't
The pattern
The rapidness
The depth
The erratic nature of it
When it all comes crashing down
The breath reveals many things
When words are just an afterthought
Our composure is steadied
Our eyes will close to clear our head
And when that breath is taken
It'll be all we need
That silence will hang on as long as we do
And our breath will seemingly stop our world for a moment
Our bodies will return back into themselves

The Last Happy Birthday Text pt. 1

It's another year
And I'll remember how you left
Instead of being there
You'll witness my life coming back together
I'll feel your presence almost everywhere I go
Especially as the wind picks up
That shiver runs down my spine
I'll look over at you making fun of me
As I put another jacket on
But this time I'll be a little bit warmer
Knowing that your embrace is coming
As the weather changes

Cracked Candy

I can't quite escape a flavor like you
I haven't found it again
Hints of you were here and there
But the original flavor is still the best,
Your sweetness made me crave candy
So I made a visit to the candy store the next day
I got myself a lollipop
I didn't even take a step
And the lollipop fell on the asphalt

It had several cracks like veins
Shattering through its body
And even though I had caused cracked candy
I still wanted to take a bite
Because I couldn't wait to get cavities from you

Never Heavier

Your eyes have never looked heavier
Your eyes are no longer soft and true
They turned vacant and troubled
And I don't know how to help
I'm used to your ebbs
But this flow is different
This is greater than whatever is following you around
I'm used to just the two of us
And now there're three

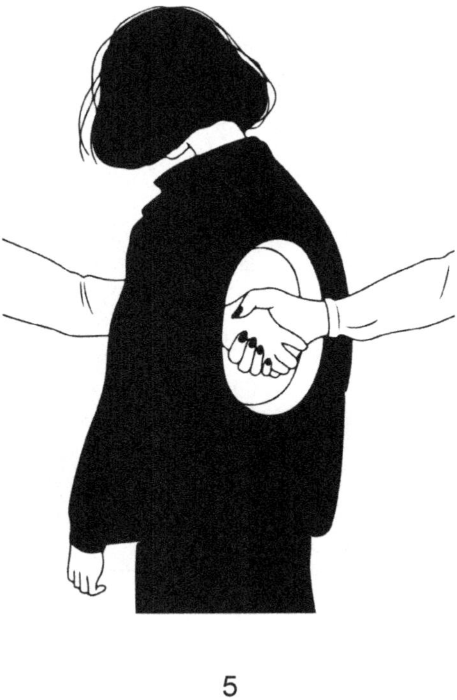

Cremated Seasons pt. 1

Look at the chorus of tears
Decorating my face
I can’t stop thinking about what I did
What I’m doing
It hurts that I still want to go back
And the tears almost looked naturally fixed
I can’t get it out of my head
Everything that happened
I want to go back

See me the way I saw you
It’s your turn to wrap yourself around my finger
Feel my pain
My self-destruction
My recklessness
And you can see me as a magnet
I can’t help it
Help me
Come back to me the way I come back to you
And we can change the decorations
Just as the seasons change

Cremated Seasons pt 2

Look at the drought on my face
A tear has not quenched my cheek in awhile
I can't stop thinking about what I did
What I'm doing
It hurts that I went back
And the tears, no longer natural
I can't get it out of my head
Everything that happened
I went back

I finally see you the way you are

I felt the pain
Fixed the self-destruction
Comforted my recklessness
And you can see me however you want
I helped myself so I don't come back to you
And I'll take down the decorations
So I can celebrate different seasons

The Silence After Love

I held him in my heart as he held me in his hands
Perhaps that's why I didn't feel secure
There was always this feeling
The ease of his absence
I was okay with that
Perhaps I thought I could take it
Everything thrown at me, all at once
If he screamed at me,
I'd let him deafen me
If he wanted to outshine the sun,
I'd let him blind me
If he wanted to suffocate me,
I'd let him silence my words, forever
But despite my senses being taken away
And I was finally left alone,
It would still make me think
I didn't do enough to keep us alive

Enough Love

I fell in love twice with the same person
Once when we were together
and the second when we weren't
I couldn't help but love the person I was with you
Because I was different
But coming out of that, I fell in love with myself
With going to the beach by myself
Going to cafes by myself
Just being by myself
Because I knew one day
It had to be enough to do all these things
And not wonder if I had made the right choice
Because I will not stay in that space, wondering
Because waking up without you will be enough

The Last Happy Birthday Text pt. 2

It's another year
And I'll remember how you came back
You saw all the pieces of my life coming together
And instead of being there
I felt your absence almost everywhere I went
Especially as the wind died down
The sun returned the warmth
I looked over at you
But this time, I wondered
If your embrace would return too

Resurfacing

It's that first inhale after resurfacing
It's the pain you feel
When you can no longer tell the temperature
Your hair is standing up for a different reason
Your lungs provoked to burn
Your body shaking out the habit
You're being called to act on this numbness, to subside it
You have many options to ease yourself back to normality
But none of them are true to what you seek
There's only one choice but to answer back
The temperature, biting at your body to react to it
And your body will carry on like it has been
But hopefully this time
Your body won't be too numb to fight back

Black World

I fiercely wrote in my notebook so much
that my pen ripped the pages
but I kept going
so much, that my whole notebook turned black,
then my room, then the world
And yet somehow the pain was still visible
I thought I could write it away
I sought for that relief
Shaking my head, I ran away leaving my notebook
But it's after me
It has one more thing to say
I didn't want to look back until my legs lost feeling
My body started shaking for relief
I felt like my lights were going out
But before I fell asleep, I turn around
My notebook's pages flashed: game over…

Mistake's Footprints

Most of the time
I don't want to feel this way
Full of scribbles and whiteouts
My mistakes don't know where to go
Up, down, under, over
Through it, a standstill
Location, location, location
Locatio
Locati
Locat
Loc
Lo
Let me try again
Most of the time
I do feel this way
Full of scribbles and whiteouts
My mistakes go to whomever they want
And I'll watch as they start fires in my life
Leaving footprints along the way

Intravenous

Lift my eyelid and you'll see white
Something had been administered directly to my heart
The same adoration of the old me
But this time, it might get to me
I could feel it surging through my veins
Fighting to feel what it use to
My body is trying to regain control of my bloodstream
Because shallow-angled lies can only go so far
When I blink, the color will return to my eyes
Along with my resolve to not go back

Rebirth

It’ll be the first thing you do
Scream out a breath, showing you're alive
And it’s the last thing you do
A sigh of relief, hopefully
To take a breath is to understand that anytime could be the last
Yet it’s not something I think about
I could give another person that chance for a first breath
And they’ll be there for my last
Hopefully

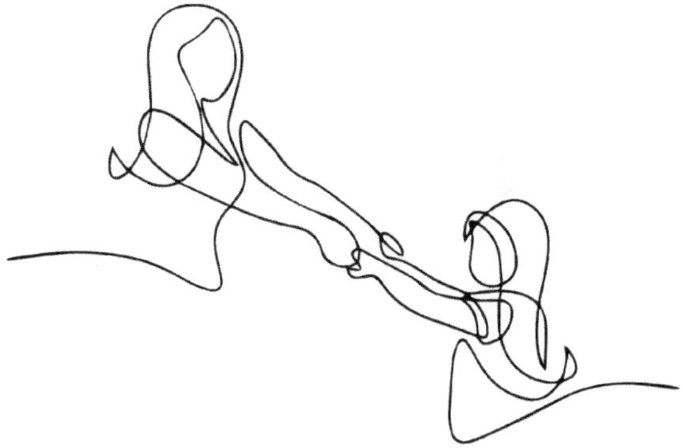

Anxiety's Wake-Up Call
pt. 1

My anxiety woke me up again today
Like I got shaken into a situation I wasn't fully aware of
Like someone had dumped an emotional crisis on me
And it was looking at me for a solution
That was normal ever since I was young
But I didn't have an answer
For years this went on
Never fully understanding the root back then
I stayed on this ride until another day started

Anxiety's Wake-Up Call pt. 2

Anxiety woke me up again
But this time it was different
It felt like it was humming
Like it was disguised as something else
Like it was warning me of something different
Of something I wouldn't know the answer to
But this time I took its hand and brought it everywhere I went
Asking myself: Is this it? Is that it?
But anxiety would shake its head
So I kept going for years
My commitment to finding a solution
Would last longer than anxiety's unwillingness to let go

So one day, I woke anxiety up
And said: it's time to go
I didn't really need to explain myself
I reached a point where anxiety was no longer a stranger
I could recognize it wherever it showed up
I could take its hand again
And I could give anxiety another chance to let go
But this time, a little quicker

Crashing Asphalt

I feel my anxious fingers find old scars
And I swear there's still asphalt in them
If I ever get ahold of a piece of one
I can point out which street it came from
And how long it took my body to recover
The older I get, the longer it took
Sometimes I'd fall so hard
I could taste the asphalt
I kind of accepted it
Somehow it'll remain of a part of me
And my memories will be scattered with the pieces
No matter how hard I try to find the flaw
I can't
And it makes me want to leave the scars alone
I would've crashed into asphalt more often if I knew
How much the impact would leave me alone in nostalgia

Well Done

I wish I could tell you how it gets better
Not *when*
Because I'd rather focus on the controllables
Than a timeline that doesn't belong to me
I can't make time go faster for me
But what I can do is accept that
All that is meant to be, will be
The good and especially the bad

All that will destroy and build me up
I welcome
Because I want to meet this woman I will ultimately become
When I do, I'll plant myself fiercely in front of the mirror and say:
Well done

Bent Sensations

And when the days have been used up
And we have gone through many sunrises
And we are bent,
Bones cracking with bandaid wrappers on the floor
Show me again, in your room at midnight
Ask if I hated it
And my eyes will answer faster than my mouth
Through it all, your touch never left
I'll scratch it off even after to feel a different
sensation
Still

My Bleeding Notebook

My notebook can take it when I can't
I'll give it my pain, my hurt
It contains the ripples of my discoveries, my growth
And some days I have to think harder
To understand what it all means
But I will write until my notebook has a heartbeat
Until the ink bleeds
Only then will I understand
why my answers are on the other side of fear

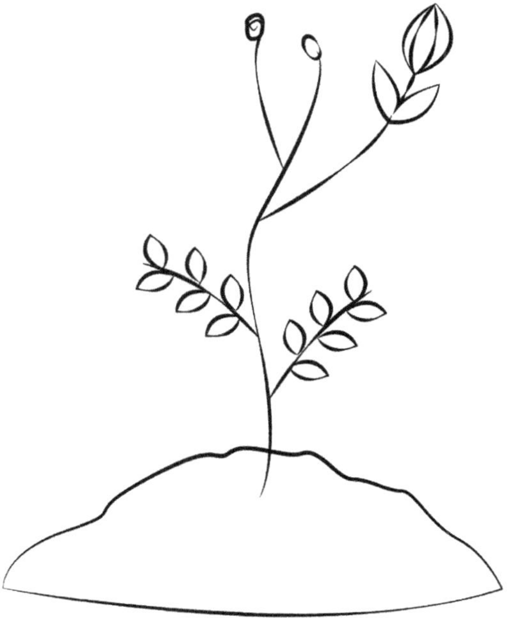

www.ingramcontent.com/pod-product-compliance
Lightning Source LLC
Chambersburg PA
CBHW051721130826
49812CB00034B/1287
* 9 7 8 9 3 5 7 4 4 1 5 8 2 *